The Dig

Dig In • Find the Treasure • Put it on Display

Volume 1 • Luke 1 – 12

Patrick Schwenk

www.thedigforkids.com

ISBN: 978-0-615-69064-3

Table of Contents

A Word to Parents

Hello, and welcome to *The Dig*!

I am a pastor, husband, and parent. Currently, my wife and I have four children ten years old and younger. My wife and I clean up spills, refill drinks, do laundry, change diapers, cut the grass, serve in ministry, drop kids off, pick kids up, take out the trash, clean the house, do more laundry – you get the point!

Like you, my wife and I wear many hats. One of the greatest joys in my life is being a dad and having the pleasure to be a pastor to my kids. My daughter said to me recently, "Dad, I am glad you are a pastor." When I asked her why, she said, "Because you teach us the Bible."

The truth is, every parent should be (and can be) a pastor to his or her children. *The Dig* has been my personal desire and attempt to teach our children the Bible from an early age.

The Apostle Paul makes an interesting comment regarding Timothy's training as a child. In 2 Timothy 3:14-15, Paul says, "But as for you, continue in what you have learned and have firmly believed, knowing from whom you learned it and **how from childhood you have been acquainted with the sacred writings,** which are able to make you wise for salvation through faith in Christ Jesus."

Paul suggests that Timothy was being taught the Bible from a very young age. *The Dig* is an effort to systematically help you as a parent study through books of the Bible so you can help your child. Out of the experience you create, biblical principles are learned and lived.

The goal, of course, is that our children will fall in love with Jesus as their Savior and grow up to follow Him with all their heart, soul, and strength. I trust that this will be a great resource for you and your family!

In Jesus,

Patrick Schwenk

About Discipleship

Before we get too far into *The Dig*, let's look at a few brief observations about teaching and training our children to be disciples of Jesus.

1. We must have the **RIGHT PICTURE** of who we want our children to be. Close your eyes for a moment and picture your son or daughter when they are 15, 25, or 35 years old. What do they look like? What do they care about? How do they pray? How do they worship? Whom do they love? As Christian parents, if the picture of our children is anything other than a disciple of Jesus, then we are aiming at the wrong target. The goal is to raise children who live, love, and serve like Jesus!

2. We must have the **RIGHT PRIORITIES**. The right picture helps us establish the right priorities. What is important to you as a parent? What do you push your children to get involved in? Why? What does success look like for you as a parent? What does success look like for your child? One of the great joys of being a parent is having the opportunity to raise children who love God. This doesn't happen by accident. It is by God's grace and our own effort to establish godly priorities.

3. We must have the **RIGHT PERSPECTIVE**. It is still God's grace that saves our children and not our best intentions or methods. With this said, keep in mind the following:

   Information: Children are often times growing up in American churches and homes less biblically literate than the previous generations. As parents, we need to be reminded of the tremendous responsibility we have to pass on the truth of God's Word.

   Impression: The goal is also to leave a positive spiritual impression on the hearts of our children. Our children won't have a pleasant memory if all they remember is Mom or Dad (tired and grouchy) drilling Bible verses into their heads! Taking your child through *The Dig* should be a memorable experience. Best lessons are taught within the context of loving and meaningful relationships.

   Imitation: Don't forget that our children listen to us and watch us. As a parent, we must be growing as a disciple of Jesus ourselves. We want to be able to say, as Paul did to the church in Corinth, "Follow me as I follow Christ" (I Corinthians 11:1).

About *The Dig*

Shortly, you will meet a character named Doc. Doc is an experienced Bible scholar and archaeologist who will be your *Dig* tour guide during each lesson. A typical *Dig* lesson follows the same pattern consisting of four main parts. Below is a short description of each of these four components.

1. **The Map**: Each lesson has a map. The map tells you and your child where you'll be going in each lesson. It is a short summary of the study ahead.

2. **The Dig**: The Dig is the main passage you will be studying. Following each passage will be several questions designed to help conversation and understanding. They are meant to be a guide. You can use them or tweak them to help you talk with your children.

3. **The Treasure**: The Treasure is the big idea of the lesson. In a short statement, it is what you want your child to remember from the passage you studied.

4. **The Display**: When an archaeologist finds a treasure, they will clean it up and put in on display for everyone to see. This is the basic idea of the Display. It is the application of the Treasure you have found. This is a great opportunity to discuss with your child how he or she can live out the truth of God's Word for everyone to see.

The Oasis is a chance to review what your child has learned so far. Make it your own and make it fun. A quiz and coloring activity are provided, and you can provide the prize! You'll also notice there are key verses in each section. Memorizing God's Word is a great way to hide God's Word in the heart of your child and also to reinforce what your son or daughter is learning.

Enjoy the adventure!

Introduction to Luke

Greetings!

Hi, I'm Doc! I've been studying the Bible, history, and archaeology for a long time. I love to learn about God's Word and teach others, too. I am very excited that you are joining me on this Bible adventure through the Gospel of Luke. You are going to be learning about who Luke was and why he wrote this book about Jesus. Most importantly, you will be learning all about Jesus as you journey through *The Dig*.

Who is the author?

Let's start by taking a look at a few interesting facts about Luke. With God's help, Luke wrote one of the books in the New Testament that we call the Gospel of Luke. Most Bible experts believe that Luke, who was a doctor and follower of Jesus, wrote this book to make sure all the facts were right about who Jesus is and what Jesus did.

Would you be mad if someone was telling other people things about you that were not true? I would be very upset! Luke wanted to make sure this didn't happen to Jesus. He wrote the Gospel of Luke so that everyone would know what was really true about Jesus.

Take a minute and see if you can find the book of Luke in your Bible. Did you find it? The first four books in the New Testament are called the gospels. They tell us about who Jesus is and what He did. The third gospel is Luke and it is the book you'll be studying very shortly. Soon, you will be a Bible expert, too!

What is the date?

Do you know when you were born? I was born in 1975. Wow, I know that is long time ago! Well, Luke wrote this book around the year 60 A.D. Now that is a really long time ago! God wanted to make sure we would never forget what He has done, so He helped people write the Bible.

Are you ready for an adventure through the Gospel of Luke? I am! Let's pray and get ready to check out our first **map**, go on a **dig**, find our **treasure**, and put God's Word on **display**!

Let's dig,

Doc

Lesson 1:
Let's Meet John the Baptist

Key Verses: Luke 1:30-31

And the angel said to her, "Do not be afraid, Mary, for you have found favor with God. And behold, you will conceive in your womb and bear a son, and you shall call his name Jesus."

The Map:

During our first lesson in Luke's gospel, we will be looking at the birth of John the Baptist. John will eventually be the one to tell everyone that Jesus is on the way! Let's take a look at how John's mom and dad find out they are going to have a new baby boy in the family. The key verses for the first six lessons are Luke 1:30-31, so don't forget to start working on memorizing!

The Dig: Luke 1:1-25

What are the names of John's parents?

Where does John's dad, Zechariah, work?

What is the temple?

How do John's parents find out they are going to have a baby?

Answer in Bible notebook

The Treasure:

God always keeps His promises! Have you ever told someone you were going to do something and then you forgot to do it? God never forgets. In the Old Testament, God had promised the Jewish people He was going to send a Savior, or Messiah, one day to forgive them of their sins and save them from their enemies. John was sent to spread the word that Jesus the Savior was on the way!

The Display:

It is never fun when someone says something and then doesn't do it. If God always does what He says, then we should, too! Is there a time someone didn't keep a promise with you? How did that make you feel?

Answer in Bible notebook

Lesson 2:
Here Comes Jesus

Key Verses: Luke 1:30-31

And the angel said to her, "Do not be afraid, Mary, for you have found favor with God. And behold, you will conceive in your womb
and bear a son, and you shall call his name Jesus."

The Map:

During this lesson, we'll be looking at how an angel announces to Joseph and Mary that Mary is going to have a baby boy. This isn't going to be just an average or ordinary boy. This is going to be a very special baby. His name will be Jesus because He is God, coming to save us from our sins and give us everlasting life!

The Dig: Luke 1:26-56

What is the name of the angel who tells Joseph and Mary about the birth of Jesus?

What is special about Jesus?

Whose family is Jesus from?

In the Old Testament, God had promised King David, the second king of Israel, that a king in his family would someday rule forever and ever. God was already letting people know about Jesus even long before in the Old Testament.

The Treasure:

The birth of Jesus is another example of how God always does what He says! God is faithful so we know we can always count on Him.

The Display:

God's people had to wait a long time for Jesus to come. They remained patient and faithful as they were waiting for God to help them. Tell me about a time you had trouble waiting for something to happen.

Lesson 3:
Jesus Is Born

Key Verses: Luke 1:30-31

And the angel said to her, "Do not be afraid, Mary, for you have found favor with God. And behold, you will conceive in your womb
and bear a son, and you shall call his name Jesus."

The Map:

When I was born, my aunt brought a brown stuffed animal to the hospital to give to me as a present. I don't remember it, but my parents told me all about it when I got older. You probably don't remember, but a lot of people came to visit you when you were born, and some even brought you presents. During this lesson, we'll be looking at the birth of Jesus. Jesus has some special visitors at His birth, too. Let's find out who they are and what they give Him!

The Dig: Luke 2:1-20

Where is Jesus born?

Who comes to visit Him?

How do they treat Jesus?

The Treasure:

Jesus is unique! He is not just another baby boy born in Israel. Jesus is God. When we look at Jesus, we are really looking at God. He came to be among us so that He could save us.

The Display:

Get the word out! When the shepherds saw Jesus, they spread the word about Him. God wants us to tell other people about who He is. Who is someone you can invite to church? Is there someone you know who isn't a Christian that you can begin praying for?

Lesson 4:
Jesus Goes to the Temple

Key Verses: Luke 1:30-31

And the angel said to her, "Do not be afraid, Mary, for you have found favor with God. And behold, you will conceive in your womb
and bear a son, and you shall call his name Jesus."

The Map:

In this lesson, we'll be looking at when Jesus goes to the temple in Jerusalem. The temple is like a church for the Jewish people. They go there to learn about God, pray, worship, and offer sacrifices for their sins. Let's take a look at what happens.

The Dig: Luke 2:21-52

How old is Jesus when His parents first take Him to the temple?

How do Simeon and Anna treat Jesus when they see Him?

When Jesus is older, what do His parents find Him doing in the temple?

The Treasure:

Jesus was wise, even as a young boy! We learn from this passage that Jesus must have really known His Bible because He was talking to the rabbis, or teachers, in the temple. They couldn't believe what He knew and how He lived even though He was young!

The Display:

Some people know a lot, but they still don't make good, or wise, choices. Wisdom isn't just about knowing a bunch of stuff. Wisdom is about obeying God. There are a lot of people who would like you to do things their way. Wisdom is knowing God's Word and living it out! What are some ways you can be wise in how you live?

Lesson 5:
John the Baptist Gets Angry

Key Verses: Luke 1:30-31

And the angel said to her, "Do not be afraid, Mary, for you have found favor with God. And behold, you will conceive in your womb
and bear a son, and you shall call his name Jesus."

The Map:

Look out because John the Baptist is upset! Why? Well, we will find out soon. In this lesson, we'll learn what John says as he is telling people that Jesus is coming.

The Dig: Luke 3:1-23

What does it mean to repent?

Why are people coming to be baptized?

Why is John upset?

Some people think John is the Messiah. What does he tell them about Jesus?

The Treasure:

Jesus gives us the power to live changed lives! John told people that when Jesus came He would give us the Holy Spirit. When we believe in Jesus, the Holy Spirit gives us the strength and power to live each day for God.

The Display:

The secret to living a changed life for Jesus isn't about trying really hard. The secret is to ask God each day to fill you with His Spirit to help you live for Him. What are some things in your life you need God's help with?

Lesson 6:
The Battle in the Desert

Key Verses: Luke 1:30-31

And the angel said to her, "Do not be afraid, Mary, for you have found favor with God. And behold, you will conceive in your womb
and bear a son, and you shall call his name Jesus."

The Map:

Do you have any enemies? An enemy is someone who doesn't like you. God created angels which are spiritual beings who don't have bodies like we do and were made to help accomplish God's plans as His messengers. The Bible tells us there was an angel who didn't want to listen to God and rebelled. We know this angel as the devil or Satan. The devil is God's enemy. In this lesson, we'll learn more about how the devil tries to stop Jesus from doing what He came to the earth to do.

The Dig: Luke 4:1-13

What is the devil trying to get Jesus to do?

How is Jesus able to stand strong against the devil?

Who wins the battle in the desert?

The Treasure:

Jesus is stronger than the devil! When we become a Christian, God gives us His Spirit so that we can win the fight against the devil, or Satan, too! Because God is stronger, there is nothing the devil can do to us that God doesn't allow.

The Display:

Living for Jesus is like being in a battle. We need to follow Jesus' example to be strong! Jesus knew God's Word and was full of God's Spirit. You can be sure that you never fight alone because Jesus has already defeated Satan by dying on the cross and rising again. What are a few ways you can be strong for Jesus?

The Oasis

Congratulations! You have made it through the first six lessons! The Oasis is a chance to stop, rest up, and review what you have learned so far on the adventure. During each Oasis, you will be quizzed over the lessons you have already done. Do you think you can remember what you have studied so far? Let's find out!

Review Key Verses: Luke 1:30-31

Take a minute and tell your mom or dad the key verses. Remember, you are not allowed to look!

Review Questions:

1. The book of Luke starts with a story about John the Baptist's parents. Do you remember their names?

2. Where does John's dad, Zechariah, work?

3. What is the name of the angel who tells Joseph and Mary about the birth of Jesus?

4. What famous king of Israel was Jesus' relative?

5. In what town is Jesus born?

6. Who comes to visit Him?

7. How old is Jesus when His parents first take Him to the temple?

8. What is John the Baptist telling people to do?

9. Whom does Jesus have a battle with in the desert?

The Oasis Activity

Draw and color a picture of what you think the angel looked like that appeared to Mary.

Lesson 7:
Jesus Is Rejected

Key Verses: Luke 5:31-32

And Jesus answered them, "Those who are well have no need of a physician, but those who are sick. I have not come to call the righteous but sinners to repentance."

The Map:

I have always wanted to be a teacher. I remember telling my parents when I was only eight years old that I wanted to be a teacher when I grew up. Sure enough, that is what I am doing! During this lesson, we'll see how teaching is a big part of Jesus' ministry. We'll look at how some people listen to Jesus and how others reject Jesus. The key verses for the next six lessons are Luke 5:31-32, so start memorizing!

The Dig: Luke 4:14-30

Where does Jesus go to teach?

In this passage, Jesus begins reading Isaiah 61. He explains it is about Him. Who is Jesus saying He is?

Does everyone believe Him?

The Treasure:

Jesus sets us free! When Jesus opened up the scrolls and read Isaiah 61, He was letting the Jewish people know He was the Messiah coming to set them free from their sins. Now that is good news!

The Display:

Even though Jesus offers us real life, some people reject Jesus because they want to do whatever they want. Do you have friends who aren't Christians? Sometimes it is hard to be a Christian because people around you might not want you to live for God. But God wants to use you to help people see how awesome living for God really is! How can you help others learn about Jesus?

Lesson 8:
Jesus Heals the Hurting

Key Verses: Luke 5:31-32

And Jesus answered them, "Those who are well have no need of a physician, but those who are sick. I have not come to call the righteous but sinners to repentance."

The Map:

Have you ever been around someone when they are sad or upset? Do you know people who are sick? In this lesson, we'll read about how Jesus helps people who are sad and heals people who are sick. Jesus is giving us a picture of what Heaven is going to be like someday! How cool is that? There will no longer be sickness, hurt, suffering, loneliness, or anything bad!

The Dig: Luke 4:31-44

What is the Sabbath?

What is a demon?

Why should Christians not be afraid of demons?

What does Jesus do to the people who are sick?

What does this tell us about Heaven?

The Treasure:

Jesus is powerful! Nothing is impossible with God. Jesus came to heal the sick and help people who were not listening to God. We don't have to be afraid because we know God is always with us. His Spirit lives in us, and gives us power to live for Him each day!

The Display:

Do people feel better or worse when they are around you? You might not be able to cure someone's sickness, but you can love him or her like Jesus did! How do you help people with your actions and words?

Lesson 9:
Jesus Calls His First Disciples

Key Verses: Luke 5:31-32

And Jesus answered them, "Those who are well have no need of a physician, but those who are sick. I have not come to call the righteous but sinners to repentance."

The Map:

A disciple is someone who wants to live for Jesus. A Christian is a disciple or follower of Jesus! In this lesson we'll learn about Jesus' first disciples. Some Bible experts believe that Jesus' followers were teenagers (12-16 years old). It doesn't matter how old you are; anyone can be a disciple!

The Dig: Luke 5:1-11

What are the names of Jesus' first disciples?

What are they doing when Jesus first calls them?

What does Jesus tell them they are going to catch instead of fish?

The Treasure:

Jesus is worth following! Everybody is following somebody. Some people look up to their favorite sports star. Some people follow what their friends at school do. Following the right person is very important. We follow God because He created us and knows what is best for us. He is worth listening to!

The Display:

Did you know your brother or sister might be watching how you act or how you talk? I'll bet you have classmates at school who watch and listen to you, too. What do they see? What do they hear? Do they see and hear someone who is living for God? I hope so! If you want to be a leader, then you first have to be a follower – a follower of Jesus, that is! How can people see Jesus by watching and listening to you?

Lesson 10:
Jesus Forgives

Key Verses: Luke 5:31-32

And Jesus answered them, "Those who are well have no need of a physician, but those who are sick. I have not come to call the righteous but sinners to repentance."

The Map:

When I was nine years old, I thought I could fool my parents by staying outside at the church playground instead of going to the service. Boy, did I get in trouble! I needed to ask my parents and God to forgive me. In this lesson, we'll learn about how Jesus not only heals people, but because He is God, He forgives sins! Our greatest need isn't to be healthy physically, but to be healthy spiritually.

The Dig: Luke 5:12-26

What does Jesus do to the man with leprosy?

How do the men get their friend to see Jesus?

Does Jesus first help the man to walk or forgive him of his sins?

Who can forgive sins? What does this teach us about Jesus?

The Treasure:

Jesus can forgive sins! The Bible says that only God can forgive sins. This passage teaches us that Jesus is God because not only can He heal people, but He can also forgive our sins. That is our greatest need.

The Display:

Jesus was always loving and serving people. As a Christian, Jesus wants us to love people like He did. But most importantly, He wants us to tell people about how Jesus can forgive sins and be with Him forever some day in Heaven. Have you ever asked Jesus to forgive you of your sins and be your Savior? Is there someone you can pray for who isn't a Christian?

Lesson 11:
Levi's Big Party

Key Verses: Luke 5:31-32

And Jesus answered them, "Those who are well have no need of a physician, but those who are sick. I have not come to call the righteous but sinners to repentance."

The Map:

Have you ever been so excited that you couldn't wait to tell someone about what happened? Well, this is what happens to Levi when he becomes a follower of Jesus. He throws a big party for his friends to hear the good news!

The Dig: Luke 5:27-32

What is Levi's job?

Do people like tax collectors?

What does Levi do after he meets Jesus?

Why are the religious leaders mad at Jesus?

Who does Jesus say He came for?

The Treasure:

Jesus loves sinners! The religious leaders got mad because Jesus was eating with sinners. But Jesus taught them that He came to save them because they really needed God.

The Display:

How should we treat people who aren't Christians? God wants us to love them and reach out to them because He wants them to be saved someday. Don't forget to love those who are really in need of God in their lives!

Lesson 12:
Jesus Wants Your Heart
(Part 1)

Key Verses: Luke 5:31-32

And Jesus answered them, "Those who are well have no need of a physician, but those who are sick. I have not come to call the righteous but sinners to repentance."

The Map:

In the next three lessons, we'll see how God wants our hearts, not just our religious activities. In other words, He wants you to really love Him, not just pretend like it. We'll see how Jesus challenges the Jewish leaders to love God with their heart, not just with their rules!

The Dig: Luke 5:33-39

Why are the Jewish leaders upset?

What does it mean to fast?

Why does Jesus say His disciples don't fast?

The Treasure:

Jesus wants our heart! Sometimes people can go to church, sing worship songs, read their Bible, pray, and even fast, and still not love God. That's the point Jesus is making. God wants us to really love Him, and not just "go through the motions."

The Display:

Take some time and talk with your mom or dad about how you show your love for God. What are some ways you have seen other people show their love for God?

The Oasis

Congratulations! You have made it through the next six lessons! The Oasis is a chance to stop, rest up, and review what you have learned so far on the adventure. During each Oasis, you will be quizzed over the lessons you have already done. Do you think you can remember what you have studied so far? Let's find out!

Review Key Verses: Luke 5:31-32

Take a minute and tell your mom or dad the key verses. Remember, you are not allowed to look!

Review Questions:

1. Where does Jesus go to teach?

2. Who is Jesus saying He is?

3. What is the Sabbath?

4. What are some of the names of Jesus' first disciples?

5. What are they doing when Jesus calls them to follow Him?

6. Who does Jesus say He came for? (Remember the story of Levi the tax collector!)

The Oasis Activity

Draw and color what kind of food you think Jesus and His friends ate at Levi's party.

Lesson 13:
Jesus Wants Your Heart
(Part 2)

Key Verse: Luke 6:31 (NIV)

Do to others as you would have them do to you.

The Map:

In this lesson, we'll see how God wants our hearts, not just our religious activities. In other words, He wants you to really love Him and not just pretend like it. Just like in the last lesson, we'll see how Jesus challenges the Jewish leaders to love God with their heart, not just their rules! The key verse for the next six lessons is Luke 6:31, so don't forget to start working on memorizing.

The Dig: Luke 6:1-5

What is the Sabbath?

What are the Pharisees, or the Jewish leaders, saying Jesus and His disciples had done?

What example does Jesus use from the Old Testament to show He hasn't broken the Law?

What else does Jesus say about Himself in verse 5?

The Treasure:

Jesus' word is greater than the religious leaders' rules! Because Jesus is God in the flesh, He is able to tell us what is right and wrong. What Jesus says has more authority over what the religious leaders say.

The Display:

God wants us to be careful about whom we listen to! God wants us to listen to Him and love Him with our all of our heart, soul, and strength. Who are the people you listen to?

Lesson 14:
Jesus Wants Your Heart
(Part 3)

Key Verse: Luke 6:31 (NIV)

Do to others as you would have them do to you.

The Map:

In this lesson, we'll see how Jesus challenges the rules of the Jewish leaders. In the last two lessons, we've been talking about how God wants us to really love Him and not just keep rules. Are you ready to dig?

The Dig: Luke 6:6-11

What do the Jewish leaders do with rules about the Sabbath?

What does Jesus do on the Sabbath?

What do the religious leaders do?

The Treasure:

God is loving and compassionate! In this passage, we see that God desires for His people to show love and kindness to people who are in need. The rules of the Jewish leaders were more important to them than showing God's compassion.

The Display:

Have you ever been too busy or distracted to help someone else out? The religious leaders were more focused on keeping the rules than they were in showing love and compassion to people in need. How can you show compassion to your friends and family?

Lesson 15:
Pray Before You Act

Key Verse: Luke 6:31 (NIV)

Do to others as you would have them do to you.

The Map:

After I graduated from high school, I decided to go to college in Israel. I wanted to study the Bible where Jesus lived. Before I made the choice to go, I prayed and prayed! It was a hard choice, but God always gives us wisdom when we ask Him. How do you make choices? Do you just do something without thinking about it? Hopefully not! In this lesson, we'll see how Jesus makes important decisions.

The Dig: Luke 6:12-16

What does Jesus go to the mountainside to do?

According to the passage, how long does Jesus pray?

What is Jesus praying about?

Take a minute and look up these Bible passages on prayer: 1 Thessalonians 5:17 and Philippians 4:6-7. What do these verses say we are supposed to do?

The Treasure:

It pays to pray! All of these verses teach us to be careful with the choices we make every day. If we are scared, we should pray. If we need wisdom, we should pray. If we are sad, we should pray. If we are thankful, we should pray. Get the point? Don't just act; always pray first!

The Display:

What are some things you want to pray for in your own life? Who are some friends or family members you can be praying for? Try to start each day this week by praying before you leave the house!

Lesson 16:
God Is with You

Key Verse: Luke 6:31 (NIV)

Do to others as you would have them do to you.

The Map:

Sometimes being a Christian can be hard! In this lesson, we'll look at Jesus' promise that even if things get rough, we have a great reward in Heaven! Do not be afraid because God is with you and loves you.

The Dig: Luke 6:17-26

Even if you are poor, hungry, insulted, crying, and even hated, what does Jesus say you are?

What do you think it means to be blessed?

What does the word "woe" mean?

The Treasure:

It's better to love God than have everything in the world! Sometimes people seem to have it all. They have lots of money, people like them, and they always seem happy. But Jesus is warning them that if they don't have a relationship with God then they really don't have true happiness!

The Display:

There is nothing better in life than knowing we have a relationship with Jesus. Even if we are poor, hungry, sad, or even hated, we know that God is with us and loves us. What makes you the happiest?

Lesson 17:
Love Your Enemies

Key Verse: Luke 6:31 (NIV)

Do to others as you would have them do to you.

The Map:

Has someone ever been mean to you? How did you treat them back? In this lesson, we'll learn about what Jesus says about our enemies. Let's get ready to dig!

The Dig: Luke 6:27-36

What is an enemy?

Do you have any enemies?

According to this passage, what does Jesus say we are supposed to do to our enemies?

Read verse 31 again. What does Jesus mean?

The Treasure:

Love is stronger than hate! Anybody can be downright nasty and mean, but not everyone can love. Jesus teaches us that the most powerful thing we can do is love people, even our enemies.

The Display:

How can you go out of your way to love someone this week? Do you know someone who isn't very nice? How can you love them?

Lesson 18:
Don't Point the Finger

Key Verse: Luke 6:31 (NIV)

Do to others as you would have them do to you.

The Map:

It's a lot easier to see what other people are doing wrong than it is to see what you are doing wrong! In this lesson, we'll see what Jesus has to say about judging other people.

The Dig: Luke 6:37-42

What does it mean to judge?

Why do you think Jesus is telling us to be careful not to judge?

What else is Jesus telling us to do?

The Treasure:

Don't make a decision about someone too quickly before you know all the facts! When you judge someone, you are looking at them and then making a decision about them. Sometimes our judgments of people are right, but sometimes they are way off. Make sure you look more closely at your own life.

The Display:

Take a minute and think about some things you think God might want you to work on changing in your own life. What are some things that you are doing or saying that you shouldn't be? Let's ask God to help with those right now!

The Oasis

Congratulations! You have made it through the next six lessons! The Oasis is a chance to stop, rest up, and review what you have learned so far on the adventure. During each Oasis, you will be quizzed over the lessons you have already done. Do you think you can remember what you have studied so far? Let's find out!

Review Key Verse: Luke 6:31 (NIV)

Take a minute and tell your mom or dad the key verse. Remember, you are not allowed to look!

Review Questions:

1. Some Jewish leaders are more concerned about _____ than they are about _____.

2. Finish this sentence: Jesus wants your _____.

3. What does Jesus go to the mountainside to do?

4. What does Jesus say about how we should treat our enemies?

5. What does it mean to judge someone?

6. Are we supposed to judge other people?

The Oasis Activity

Can you find the Golden Rule
written in your heart?

as you find each word fill it in

— — — — — — — —

— — — — — —

LUKE 6:31

Lesson 19:
Who Wants a Rotten Apple?

Key Verse: Luke 6:43

For no good tree bears bad fruit,
nor again does a bad tree bear good fruit.

The Map:

Have you ever picked a piece of fruit off of a tree? One time when I was hiking up to Masada, a mountain overlooking the Sea of Galilee, I stopped to pick a piece of fruit from a branch that was hanging over a fence. When I bit into what I thought was going to be a juicy apple, it turned out to be rotten! Boy, was I surprised. In this lesson, we'll learn what Jesus says about rotten fruit. The key verse for the next six lessons is Luke 6:43, so start memorizing!

The Dig: Luke 6:43-45

What can't a good tree do?

What can't a bad tree do?

What do you think Jesus is teaching us?

The Treasure:

A bad tree will grow bad fruit, but a good tree will grow good fruit. Which tree do you want to be like? A good person does good things, but a bad heart produces bad actions (fruit).

The Display:

Remember a few lessons ago when we talked about how Jesus wants our hearts? Jesus is saying that when we really love God with everything we have then we will do the right thing. We will be like a good tree that produces good fruit. If our hearts don't love and believe God, we will be like a bad tree that produces rotten fruit! What are examples of good fruit?

Lesson 20:
Where Are YOU Going to Build?

Key Verse: Luke 6:43

For no good tree bears bad fruit,
nor again does a bad tree bear good fruit.

The Map:

Have you ever built something and then it came crashing down? In this lesson, we'll be looking at two different ways to build. You can either build on sand or build on the Rock. Let's dig!

The Dig: Luke 6:46-49

What kind of foundation does the first builder build on?

What about the second?

Why does the second house come crashing down?

What is Jesus trying to teach us through this story?

The Treasure:

Jesus wants us to do what He says! If we obey Jesus, we will be like a house built on a solid foundation. People who don't listen to Jesus build their lives on sand. Be careful who you listen to!

The Display:

Jesus wants your heart! He wants you to listen and obey because He loves you. He doesn't want you take make unwise choices and hurt your life. Jesus wants you to be strong and do the right thing. Can you think of a few things Jesus wants you to do? Pray about these and ask God to help you listen and obey!

Lesson 21:
Great Faith

Key Verse: Luke 6:43

For no good tree bears bad fruit,
nor again does a bad tree bear good fruit.

The Map:

How often do you sit down on a chair only after you make sure the legs aren't broken? Each time you sit down you are trusting the chair is strong and sturdy. You are trusting the chair is going to hold you up and not come crashing down. In this lesson, we'll be learning about having faith and trust in God. Are you ready to dig?

The Dig: Luke 7:1-10

What is wrong with the centurion's servant?

What does the centurion do?

What does he want Jesus to do?

Take another look at verse 9. How does Jesus respond?

Check out Hebrews 11:1 and 11:6. Why do you think it pleases God to have faith in Him?

The Treasure:

Jesus is amazed with our faith! He wants us to know Him, trust Him, and then obey Him. Having faith is loving and obeying God no matter what happens even when things are tough. The Lord is always with us and He wants us to put our faith in Him always!

The Display:

How do you show you believe in God and have a relationship with Him?

Lesson 22:
Dead Man Talking

Key Verse: Luke 6:43

For no good tree bears bad fruit,
nor again does a bad tree bear good fruit.

The Map:

Dead man talking? What? In this lesson, we'll see how Jesus performs another amazing miracle to prove that He is who He claims to be. He even has power to bring the dead to life again!

The Dig: Luke 7:11-17

What is wrong with the widow's son?

Take another look at verse 13. How does Jesus feel when He sees her?

What does Jesus do then?

When Jesus heals her son, what do the people say about Jesus in verse 16?

The Treasure:

Jesus is stronger than death! As we've seen, He has the power to heal the sick, the lame, and even raise the dead. God is amazing!

The Display:

Jesus was always showing love and compassion to people who were hurting or in need. How can you show your friends or family love and compassion?

Lesson 23:
Jesus the Messiah

Key Verse: Luke 6:43

For no good tree bears bad fruit,
nor again does a bad tree bear good fruit.

The Map:

Have you ever waited a long time for something? It's not fun to wait! The Jewish people had been waiting a long time for the Messiah, or Savior, to come and save them from their enemies. In this lesson, we'll see how Jesus teaches that He is the Messiah who has come to save them, and us, from sin!

The Dig: Luke 7:18-35

We learned about John the Baptist in the first few lessons. Do you remember what he does?

In the passage we just read, what is John the Baptist trying to make sure of?

In verses 22 and 23, what does Jesus tell His disciples to tell John?

What is Jesus saying about Himself?

The Treasure:

Jesus is our Messiah and Savior! We could never be perfect enough to make God love us, but God showed us how amazing His love really is by sending Jesus to forgive us of our sins so we could have a relationship with Him. God loved us first and now we want to love Him back!

The Display:

Have you ever received an amazing gift? What did you do? How is Jesus an amazing gift from God?

Lesson 24:
Expensive Perfume at the Feet of Jesus

Key Verse: Luke 6:43

For no good tree bears bad fruit,
nor again does a bad tree bear good fruit.

The Map:

Have you ever done something and you knew you were going to be in big trouble? In this lesson, we are going to read and talk about a woman who has lived a sinful life and had done a lot of bad things, but she also knows that Jesus can forgive her of it all. Let's check out the story!

The Dig: Luke 7:36-50

Who invites Jesus over for dinner?

Who else comes to the dinner to see Jesus?

What does she do? Why does Jesus say she is doing this?

What does Jesus say to her?

The Treasure:

Jesus can forgive any sin! Even though this woman had done a lot of bad things, when she came to Jesus, He loved her so much that He forgave her of all her sin. This made her love Jesus even more!

The Display:

Some people think you can only be forgiven from your sins by doing good deeds, but the Bible says the only way to be forgiven for our sins is by believing in Jesus! Now, because Jesus was willing to forgive us, we should be willing to forgive other people when they hurt our feelings. Explain a time when you had to forgive a friend or family member. How did you do it?

The Oasis

Congratulations! You have made it through the next six lessons! The Oasis is a chance to stop, rest up, and review what you have learned so far on the adventure. During each Oasis, you will be quizzed over the lessons you have already done. Do you think you can remember what you have studied so far? Let's find out!

Review Key Verse: Luke 6:43

Take a minute and tell your mom or dad the key verse. Remember, you are not allowed to look!

Review Questions:

1. How does Jesus say you can tell if a tree is a good tree or bad tree?

2. Jesus tells a story about a builder. What are the two kinds of foundations the builder built on?

3. Who is the Rock?

4. How do we build our life on Jesus' words?

5. What does Jesus do for the widow's son who has died?

6. Who are the Jewish people waiting for?

The Oasis Activity

Draw and color the fruit being picked
from the tree above.

Lesson 25:
A Farmer Goes Out
Throwing Seed

Key Verse: Luke 8:15

As for that in the good soil, they are those who, hearing the word, hold it fast in an honest and good heart, and bear fruit with patience.

The Map:

Have you ever planted something? Did it grow? One time when I was in Israel I tried growing an apple tree. I waited for three months and never saw a tree or an apple. I guess I am a better Bible scholar than farmer! In this lesson, Jesus is going to tell a story about a farmer. Let's find out what happened to this farmer and what he wanted to grow. The key verse is Luke 8:15, so don't forget to start working on memorizing!

The Dig: Luke 8:1-15

What does the farmer throw?

Does all of the seed grow? What happens to it?

What kind of soil does the seed end up growing on?

What does Jesus say the good soil is like? Check out verse 15.

The Treasure:

A good heart is like good soil! As Christians, we need to have a heart that listens to God's Word and then obeys. A bad heart is when we know what the Bible teaches, but then choose not to obey.

The Display:

So far we've seen how Jesus wants us to be like a good tree that bears fruit and now we've seen how Jesus wants us to be like good soil. What are some examples of how you can learn to have a good heart?

Lesson 26:
Let Your Light Shine

Key Verse: Luke 8:15

As for that in the good soil, they are those who, hearing the word, hold it fast in an honest and good heart, and bear fruit with patience.

The Map:

Have you ever been in a really dark place where you couldn't see and no one could see you? That can be pretty scary! In this lesson, we'll learn that as Christians, Jesus wants us to be light in the darkness. Let's dig!

The Dig: Luke 8:16-21

What does Jesus say no one does?

What is Jesus saying?

What is Jesus saying we are?

How are we light?

The Treasure:

Jesus wants us to be like a light in a dark room. He wants us as His followers to help get rid of the darkness around us!

The Display:

Can you think of some examples of darkness at your school? Maybe it's the kids who pick on other kids, the students who don't do their best, or the students who don't treat one another or their teachers with respect. How can you be light everywhere you go?

Lesson 27:
Jesus Calms a Crazy Storm

Key Verse: Luke 8:15

As for that in the good soil, they are those who, hearing the word, hold it fast in an honest and good heart, and bear fruit with patience.

The Map:

Do you like storms? When I was young, I was really afraid of thunder and lightning! In this lesson, we are going to read a story about Jesus' disciples being frightened during a really bad storm.

The Dig: Luke 8:22-25

Where are Jesus and His disciples going?

What happens when they are on the boat?

What do the disciples do?

What does Jesus say to them in verse 25?

The Treasure:

Jesus wants us to keep our eyes on Him and not on the storm! It's easy to get scared in life when bad things are happening. Jesus is teaching us that He is in control of all things, so don't fear! Even when life feels like a big scary storm, God is still in control. Keep your eyes on Him!

The Display:

What are you afraid of? What do you do when you are afraid? Let's take a minute and pray for some of those fears. God doesn't want us to live in fear. He wants us to have faith in Him. We can trust God no matter what because we know He is good and He loves us!

Lesson 28:
Jesus Sets a Man Free

Key Verse: Luke 8:15

As for that in the good soil, they are those who, hearing the word, hold it fast in an honest and good heart, and bear fruit with patience.

The Map:

Has someone ever done something really nice for you? How did you treat that person? In this lesson, we'll learn about how a man was set free by Jesus and he couldn't help but tell others about it.

The Dig: Luke 8:26-39

What is wrong with the man in this story?

What does Jesus do to the demons that are controlling this man?

How do some of the people who are watching respond?

In verse 38, what does the man want to do? What does Jesus tell him to do?

The Treasure:

Jesus gives us real life! This poor guy was miserable because he wasn't living for God, but everything changed when Jesus set him free. Boy, was he thankful, too!

The Display:

Jesus doesn't want you to keep quiet about what He has done for you. Don't be afraid to tell God or tell others about how awesome He is! What are you thankful to God for? What has God done for you that you can praise Him for?

Lesson 29:
Jesus Is Never Too Busy

Key Verse: Luke 8:15

As for that in the good soil, they are those who, hearing the word, hold it fast in an honest and good heart, and bear fruit with patience.

The Map:

You have made it to the last lesson in Luke 8. We'll see how Jesus is on His way to heal someone when something very unusual happens. Do you have any guesses? We'll see what it is!

The Dig: Luke 8:40-56

Jesus is on His way to help whom?

What happens when He is on the way?

Is Jesus too busy to help her?

What does He do for her?

The Treasure:

Jesus is never too busy to help others. Even though Jesus was in a hurry to get somewhere, He still stopped to help the woman who came to Him. That is amazing!

The Display:

Jesus shows us how we as Christians should always be willing and ready to help other people, even if we are in a hurry. People matter to God and they should matter to us! How do you act when someone asks you for help? Do you have a good attitude or a bad attitude? What are some ways you can help others who are in need?

Lesson 30:
Go Do What I Do

Key Verse: Luke 8:15

As for that in the good soil, they are those who, hearing the word, hold it fast in an honest and good heart, and bear fruit with patience.

The Map:

Have you ever wanted help with something? What was it? In this lesson, we'll learn how Jesus wants the help of His disciples, or followers, to get the word out about God's amazing love.

The Dig: Luke 9:1-9

What does Jesus give His disciples so they can get the word out?

Why does Jesus tell His disciples not to take a bag, food, or money?

Are Jesus' disciples always accepted and welcomed?

The Treasure:

Jesus wants your help! Have you ever been so excited about something you couldn't help but get the word out? Jesus wants our help to let other people know how amazing God's love is for them. Just like He sent out the first twelve disciples, He is also sending us out to tell other people about God.

The Display:

Don't be afraid to tell other people about God's amazing love. And don't forget that God will provide for all of your needs! Do you have friends you can invite to church? Who are some friends you can pray for who you know are not living for God right now?

The Oasis

Congratulations! You have made it through the next six lessons! The Oasis is a chance to stop, rest up, and review what you have learned so far on the adventure. During each Oasis, you will be quizzed over the lessons you have already done. Do you think you can remember what you have studied so far? Let's find out!

Review Key Verse: Luke 8:15

Take a minute and tell your mom or dad the key verse. Remember, you are not allowed to look!

Review Questions:

1. What does the woman with expensive perfume do for Jesus?

2. Why does she love Him so much?

3. What happens to the disciples when they are in the boat?

4. What does Jesus do for the woman who asks for help?

5. What is Jesus never too busy to do?

The Oasis Activity

Draw and color what the plants may
look like from each type of soil

Lesson 31:
I'm Confused

Key Verse: Luke 9:23

And he said to all, "If anyone would come after me, let him deny himself and take up his cross daily and follow me."

The Map:

Have you ever been confused about something? In this lesson, we'll learn about how Herod doesn't understand who Jesus is. He thinks Jesus might be John the Baptist or even Elijah, one of the prophets of Israel. Let's take a look! The key verse for the next six lessons is Luke 9:23, so don't forget to start working on memorizing.

The Dig: Luke 9:7-9; Matthew 14:1-12

Why does Herod not like John the Baptist?

What happens to John?

In Luke 9:9, what does it say Herod keeps trying to do?

The Treasure:

We need to help people see Jesus! Some people don't want to know more about Jesus, but some people do. We know that everyone needs to know Jesus! One of the best things we can do as His disciples is to help them see what Jesus is like.

The Display:

How do you think we help people see Jesus? What are some ways you can be more like Jesus?

Lesson 32:
Jesus Feeds the Five Thousand

Key Verse: Luke 9:23

And he said to all, "If anyone would come after me, let him deny himself and take up his cross daily and follow me."

The Map:

Have you ever been really hungry but had nothing to eat? We are going to read a story about how Jesus' disciples help feed thousands of people with just a little bit of food. They think they don't have enough, but Jesus showed them that anything is possible with God!

The Dig: Luke 9:10-17

What do the disciples say is wrong with the crowds?

Look at verse 13. Who does Jesus say He wants to feed the crowds?

What is the problem?

Do they end up having enough food to feed everyone?

The Treasure:

God can do something big even with something small! Even though the disciples only had five loaves of bread and two fish, with God's help, thousands of people got to eat. That is amazing!

The Display:

Did you know that even the little things we do or say God may use to make a big difference in someone else's life? God wants us to obey Him even in the little things, like encouraging a friend or relative with your words or giving some of your money away to someone in need instead of buying a new toy. How about offering to pray for someone at school who looks like they are sad? These seem like little things, but God can use them in a big way if you let Him!

Lesson 33:
Real Life

Key Verse: Luke 9:23

And he said to all, "If anyone would come after me, let him deny himself and take up his cross daily and follow me."

The Map:

In this lesson, we'll look at how Jesus is warning His disciples that He is going to die for their sins soon. We'll see how He is teaching them that living for Him is the most important thing we can do. Let's dig!

The Dig: Luke 9:21-27

What does Jesus say is going to happen to Him soon?

What do you think Jesus means when He says, "What do you benefit if you gain the whole world but are yourself lost or destroyed?"

What does it mean to be ashamed of Jesus?

The Treasure:

Real life is found in living for Jesus! Some people think they will be happy if they have a huge house, fancy sports car, lots of money, or cool clothes. But Jesus says we can have all of those things and still not be happy. In fact, all of those things don't last – only Jesus does!

The Display:

Don't chase after the wrong things! The most important thing you can do in life is live for Jesus. Jesus is teaching us we need to live for Him each day. Life isn't just about what we want. It's about loving God and loving people! How do you show that you are living for Jesus each day?

Lesson 34:
We Really Saw Jesus

Key Verse: Luke 9:23

And he said to all, "If anyone would come after me, let him deny himself and take up his cross daily and follow me."

The Map:

In this lesson, we'll learn about a time when Jesus and three of His closest disciples went up on a mountain to pray. Peter, James, and John were never the same after what their eyes saw! Let's take a look and see what happened.

The Dig: Luke 9:28-36

Where do Jesus and His disciples go?

Who is on top of the mountain?

Why do you think it is significant that Moses and Elijah were there?

Read Luke 9:32 again. What does it say the disciples saw?

The Treasure:

Do you think Peter, James, and John were different because of how they saw Jesus? Jesus doesn't want us to see Him as just another ordinary person. He wants us to see Him for who He really is – our Savior!

The Display:

Jesus is worth following and loving. Some people see sports, video games, or friends as more important than living for God. But when we really see who Jesus is and what He has done for us, He becomes the main thing in our lives! What is most important to you?

Lesson 35:
Jesus Beats the Devil Again

Key Verse: Luke 9:23

And he said to all, "If anyone would come after me, let him deny himself and take up his cross daily and follow me."

The Map:

In Luke 8, we read about how Jesus has power over all Creation and the wind and the waves obey Him. If you remember way back in Luke 4, we saw that Jesus is stronger than the devil! As Christians, we don't need to fear the devil or demons because Jesus protects us. We'll see in this lesson how Jesus protects a boy who is being hurt by a demon.

The Dig: Luke 9:37-45

In the passage we just read, what is happening to the boy?

Do you remember what the Bible says a demon or evil spirit is?

As Christians, can demons hurt us?

Look again at verse 41. Why does Jesus get upset?

The Treasure:

Jesus is our protector! There is nothing in the whole world that is stronger or more powerful than God. This is why it's so important for us to follow Jesus. He has promised to always be with us and help us no matter what is going on in our lives.

The Display:

Do you ever get scared or feel sad? Don't forget that Jesus died and rose again for you. Remember that when you became a Christian, the Holy Spirit now lives in you. God is always with you! He doesn't want us to doubt that He is powerful enough to help anyone! He wants us to have faith in Him. What are things in your life that you are worried about right now? Take some time and pray with your mom and dad. Ask God to help you remember that He is with you and He is on your side!

Lesson 36:
Who Is the Greatest?

Key Verse: Luke 9:23

And he said to all, "If anyone would come after me, let him deny himself and take up his cross daily and follow me."

The Map:

Some people want everyone to see how cool they are or how good they are at a sport or in school. They like being the center of attention! Do you know anyone like this? In this lesson, we will see how Jesus wants His followers to act. Let's dig!

The Dig: Luke 9:46-50

What are the disciples doing in this passage? Why?

Who does Jesus say is the greatest? If you can't remember, check out the last sentence in verse 48.

What do you think Jesus means by the least?

The Treasure:

Help people see Jesus, not just you! The best thing we can do in life is not show people how amazing we are, but to help them see how amazing God is! He is the greatest! When we are following Jesus and loving people we are showing them how great God really is.

The Display:

Can you think of some ways that people try to show how great they are? How can you show how great Jesus is? Take some time and pray about helping others see more of Jesus living through you!

The Oasis

Congratulations! You have made it through the next six lessons! The Oasis is a chance to stop, rest up, and review what you have learned so far on the adventure. During each Oasis, you will be quizzed over the lessons you have already done. Do you think you can remember what you have studied so far? Let's find out!

Review Key Verse: Luke 9:23

Take a minute and tell your mom or dad the key verse. Remember, you are not allowed to look!

Review Questions:

1. Why does Herod not like John the Baptist?

2. What does Jesus ask the disciples to do when He sees the crowds without food?

3. What does it mean to be ashamed of Jesus?

4. What does the Bible say a demon is?

5. As Christians, can demons hurt us?

The Oasis Activity

Day in and day out we live a life about the cross
trace a path in and out of the maze around the cross

Lesson 37:
James and John
Call Down Fire

Key Verse: Luke 10:33

But a Samaritan, as he journeyed, came to where he was, and when he saw him, he had compassion.

The Map:

In this lesson, we'll learn about how James and John asks Jesus for a rather silly request. Jesus is not really happy about what they are asking for. Let's see what James and John want to do! The key verse is Luke 10:33, so don't forget to start working on memorizing.

The Dig: Luke 9:51-56

Where is Jesus walking?

Are the people in the Samaritan village nice to Jesus, James, and John?

What do James and John ask Jesus if they can do? Take a look at 2 Kings 1:10-12.

What does Jesus say to them?

The Treasure:

Loving is better than being mean! Since James and John were mad, they called down fire on the Samaritans to get back at them. Jesus was showing them how we don't fight back with fire, but instead, with love!

The Display:

When someone is mean to us, we sometimes want to get back at that person by being unkind to them. Is this what Jesus wants us to do? No way! Jesus teaches us that we should always do our best to love people and be kind to them even if they aren't kind back. Do you remember a time when someone was mean to you? How did you react?

Lesson 38:
The Cost of Following Jesus

Key Verse: Luke 10:33

But a Samaritan, as he journeyed, came to where he was, and when he saw him, he had compassion.

The Map:

In this lesson, we'll learn about how following Jesus can be hard. It isn't always easy to obey God, but it is always the best thing for us because we know God loves us. It is better to follow Jesus than to follow what everyone else is doing!

The Dig: Luke 9:57-62

What does the first man say to Jesus?

What does the second man say?

What does the third man say?

At the very end of these verses, Jesus is basically saying, "Don't look back!" What do you think Jesus means?

The Treasure:

Don't quit! Each of these men said they wanted to follow Jesus except for when it got hard. Jesus is teaching us in this passage that we need to keep going and not take our eyes off Jesus!

The Display:

Have you ever run in a race? What did you do when you got tired? I'll bet there were times when you were running that you wanted to stop or quit the race. Jesus wants to remind us that we need to keep our eyes on Him and keep running!

Lesson 39:
Give Me Real Joy

Key Verse: Luke 10:33

But a Samaritan, as he journeyed, came to where he was, and when he saw him, he had compassion.

The Map:

Ever since Jesus first called His disciples to follow Him, He has been teaching them how to live for God. Now He is going to send a lot of His disciples out to different towns and villages to share the good news! Let's take a look and see what happens.

The Dig: Luke 10:1-20

How many disciples does Jesus send out to share the good news?

Does Jesus promise that everyone would welcome the disciples?

How does Jesus teach them to respond to people who don't want to hear about Jesus?

Look at verse 17 again. What kind of attitude do the disciples have when they return?

The Treasure:

Obeying God is the only way to get real joy! Some people try to find joy and happiness by buying lots of stuff, having lots of money, doing things that aren't good for them or having certain friends. Jesus reminds us that living for God is the only way to have real joy!

The Display:

There are a lot of things in life that can make us happy. We need to have the right friends. We need to have money for food, clothes, and a home. It's okay to have fun watching a movie or playing games, but none of these things can take the place of obeying God. Take a few moments and discuss with your mom or dad why only God can give us the joy we really need.

Lesson 40:
Help

Key Verse: Luke 10:33

But a Samaritan, as he journeyed, came to where he was, and when he saw him, he had compassion.

The Map:

About five years ago, I was driving through the wilderness between Egypt and southern Israel. My jeep broke down because it was so hot. I waited for three hours until someone finally stopped to help me, and I was so grateful they stopped. In this lesson, we are going to study a parable where Jesus tells us about stopping and helping the hurting.

The Dig: Luke 10:25-37

What happens to the man going from Jerusalem to Jericho?

What does the priest do when he sees the man injured on the side of the road?

What does the Levite do when he sees the injured man?

What does the Samaritan do?

Which one of these men is a good friend and neighbor?

The Treasure:

Help the hurting! In Jesus' parable, two of the men just walked right by the injured man on the side of the road, but the Samaritan man stopped and helped the hurting man. He was a good friend because he cared enough to help!

The Display:

Why do you think the two men didn't stop to help? What made the Samaritan stop to help? What are some ways you can be like the Samaritan man in the parable that Jesus told?

Lesson 41:
Worshippers and Workers

Key Verse: Luke 10:33

But a Samaritan, as he journeyed, came to where he was, and when he saw him, he had compassion.

The Map:

In this lesson, we'll be looking at how two different women responded to Jesus when He came to their house. What would you do if Jesus came to your house? We'll see how one of the women is a worshipper and the other is a worker. Let's read the story and find out what we can learn!

The Dig: Luke 10:38-42

What are the names of the two sisters?

What does Martha do when Jesus comes to their house?

What does Mary do?

Take a minute and look up the following verses: Luke 10:39, John 11:32, and John 12:3. What is Mary doing in each of these verses?

The Treasure:

Jesus wants us to worship Him before we work for Him! Martha was distracted and ignored Jesus. Imagine having Jesus in your house and then leaving Him to go play in your room! But Mary wanted to be with Jesus and learn from Him. Mary understood that it is important to worship Jesus and work for Him. First, we must spend time worshipping Him and then we can live for Him!

The Display:

Do you enjoy spending time with your friends? This is how Jesus wants us to feel about spending time worshipping Him! What does it mean to worship Jesus? What does it mean to work for Jesus?

Lesson 42:
Pray the Right Way

Key Verses: Luke 10:33

But a Samaritan, as he journeyed, came to where he was, and when he saw him, he had compassion.

The Map:

When I was in college, I really wanted to take a trip to Egypt but I didn't have enough money to go. I prayed and prayed, but I couldn't save enough money. Boy, was I sad! I realized that sometimes I can pray for the wrong things even if they seem like good things. In this lesson, we'll see how Jesus taught His disciples to pray.

The Dig: Luke 11:1-13

What do Jesus' disciples ask Him to do?

Whom does Jesus say we are to pray to?

What are some things Jesus mentioned we should ask God the Father for?

Does Jesus say we should give up if our prayers aren't answered right away?

The Treasure:

Prayer should be a priority! God wants us to remember that praying to Him is very important because He is a loving Father. He doesn't always give us what we think we need, but He does give us what is best for us. Jesus is reminding us that when we pray we should always pray for what God wants, not just what we want!

The Display:

Prayer is simply talking to God. When do you like to pray the most? What are some things you can pray for?

The Oasis

Congratulations! You have made it through the next six lessons! The Oasis is a chance to stop, rest up, and review what you have learned so far on the adventure. During each Oasis, you will be quizzed over the lessons you have already done. Do you think you can remember what you have studied so far? Let's find out!

Review Key Verse: Luke 10:33

Take a minute and tell your mom or dad the key verse. Remember, you are not allowed to look!

Review Questions:

1. Who does Jesus say is the greatest?

2. What do James and John ask Jesus if they can do?

3. What does Jesus say to them?

4. How many disciples does Jesus send out to share the good news?

5. Does Jesus promise that everyone would welcome them or be nice to them?

6. What happens to the man traveling from Jerusalem to Jericho?

7. What does the Samaritan do for the injured man?

The Oasis Activity

Color the picture of the Good Samaritan having compassion on the
injured traveler.

Lesson 43:
Whose Team Are You On?

Key Verses: Luke 12:22-23

And he said to his disciples, "Therefore I tell you, do not be anxious about your life, what you will eat, nor about your body, what you will put on. For life is more than food, and the body more than clothing."

The Map:

If you have ever played in a game of basketball or football, you know that you can't play on both teams at the same time. You are either on one team or the other. In this lesson, Jesus was teaching the religious leaders that you have to pick which team you are going to be on! The key verses for the last section are Luke 12:22-23, so start memorizing!

The Dig: Luke 11:14-28

What is Jesus doing that causes the religious leaders to get upset?

Whose power do they say Jesus was using to help people?

Whose power does Jesus say He was using to defeat evil?

Read verse 28. Who are the people that Jesus said are on God's team?

The Treasure:

God wants us to fight against evil in the world, not be a part of it! The Bible teaches that Satan is always trying to mess up what good God is doing in the world. This started all the way back in the Garden of Eden. Remember what the Serpent did to Adam and Eve? But Jesus has defeated Satan and God wants us to join Him by listening and obeying!

The Display:

The religious leaders rejected that Jesus was from God. They didn't want to listen or obey Jesus. Sometimes we need help obeying God, too. Fortunately, God loves us and forgives us when we sin. How do you need help listening and obeying Jesus this week? Take some time right now and pray that God would help you listen and obey Him!

Lesson 44:
Show Us a Sign

Key Verses: Luke 12:22-23

And he said to his disciples, "Therefore I tell you, do not be anxious about your life, what you will eat, nor about your body, what you will put on. For life is more than food, and the body more than clothing."

The Map:

Do you like to collect baseball or football cards? Maybe you like to collect a favorite kind of toy? When I was in the fourth grade, my best friend loved baseball cards. One day he told me he had a very expensive Ricky Henderson baseball card. I was not going to believe him until I saw it with my own eyes! In this lesson, we're going to read about some people who kept asking Jesus to prove that He was the Messiah, God's Savior. Let's take a look at what Jesus says to them!

The Dig: Luke 11:29-32

What does Jesus say the people keep asking for?

What sign does Jesus say He will give them?

Do you remember what happened to Jonah? If you need a reminder, take a minute and read Jonah 1:15-17.

The Treasure:

Don't be a doubter! The people wanted more and more "signs" to prove that He really was the Savior of the world. Jesus was teaching them that He is greater than Jonah and Solomon because He takes away our sins and gives us real life!

The Display:

The writer of Hebrews says, "Faith is being sure of what we hope for and certain of what we do not see" (Hebrews 11:1). What are ways you show you believe in Jesus? How do you show other people you have faith in Jesus?

Lesson 45:
Who Turned Out the Lights?

Key Verses: Luke 12:22-23

And he said to his disciples, "Therefore I tell you, do not be anxious about your life, what you will eat, nor about your body, what you will put on. For life is more than food, and the body more than clothing."

The Map:

Have you ever been in a really dark place with no light? It is pretty scary! Light helps us and others see in the dark. In this lesson, we'll be looking at just a few verses about light and darkness. Let's dig!

The Dig: Luke 11:33-36

What does Jesus say no one does? Look at verse 33.

What happens when you cover up a light?

Take a moment and read John 8:12. What does Jesus say about Himself? What does He say about people who follow Him?

Read Psalm 119:105. What does this say about God's Word, the Bible?

The Treasure:

Jesus is the Light of the world and His disciples are called to be light to the world. When you become a Christian, you begin to follow what Jesus says. Living without Him is like walking through the desert with no flashlight. Jesus and His Word help us to know Him and live for Him each day. We don't have to be afraid because God is with us and leading us. Keep your eyes on Jesus!

The Display:

Take a moment and read Matthew 5:14. Jesus wants us to be "light" to our family, friends, classmates, and neighbors. What are some ways you can be light to your friends or family?

Lesson 46:
Woe to You

Key Verses: Luke 12:22-23

And he said to his disciples, "Therefore I tell you, do not be anxious about your life, what you will eat, nor about your body, what you will put on. For life is more than food, and the body more than clothing."

The Map:

Have you ever gotten really mad at someone because they weren't doing what they said they were going to do? In this lesson, we will look at how Jesus got pretty upset at the religious leaders in Jerusalem, the Pharisees, because they weren't doing what they said they would do.

The Dig: Luke 11:37:54

What word does Jesus use over and over again in this passage?

Take a minute and count how many times Jesus says, "Woe!" Why does He use the word "woe"?

What are the Pharisees doing wrong?

The Treasure:

Jesus wants us to be real! The Pharisees were saying one thing and doing another. On the outside, it looked like they loved God, but on the inside, they were being pretty mean and selfish. Some people go to church, read their Bibles, pray, and sing worship songs because they have to. God wants us to love Him because we want to!

The Display:

One of the problems with the Pharisees is that they thought God loved them because of how good they were being. We can't save ourselves by our good deeds. All of us sin and that is why we need Jesus. It's not what we do that saves us; it is what Jesus has done for us! Take a couple of minutes and talk with your mom and dad about what you are most thankful to God for.

Lesson 47:
It's Better to Please God

Key Verses: Luke 12:22-23

And he said to his disciples, "Therefore I tell you, do not be anxious about your life, what you will eat, nor about your body, what you will put on. For life is more than food, and the body more than clothing."

The Map:

When I was growing up, I used to be really afraid of the dark. I was also scared of snakes. What are you afraid of? In this lesson, we are going to read about something Jesus told His disciples not to be afraid of. Let's dig!

The Dig: Luke 12:1-12

Who do you think Jesus is telling His disciples not to be afraid of?

Who does Jesus tell us to fear? Take another look at verse 5.

Why does Jesus tell us not to fear people?

The Treasure:

It is better to please God than to please people! Jesus was warning His disciples that some people would be mean to them and even try to kill them. Jesus was teaching His disciples and us that God is more powerful than people. Don't worry about what people think of you because you are a Christian. It is better to do what is right and live for God. Be strong and courageous because God is with you and loves you!

The Display:

Are there things you are worried about or afraid of right now? God doesn't want you to worry and be scared. He wants you to know He is always with you and will help you get though anything. What do you need to ask God to help you with right now?

Lesson 48:
Don't Be Greedy

Key Verses: Luke 12:22-23

And he said to his disciples, "Therefore I tell you, do not be anxious about your life, what you will eat, nor about your body, what you will put on. For life is more than food, and the body more than clothing."

The Map:

Have you ever met someone who doesn't like to share? I grew up with two older sisters and I never liked to let them play with my toys. I didn't know I was being greedy! In this lesson, we are going to learn about what Jesus says about our stuff. Jesus is going to tell a parable about someone who had lots of money and only wanted more. Let's dig!

The Dig: Luke 12:13-21

What does Jesus tell us to watch out for? Look at verse 15.

What do you think greed is?

What does the man in Jesus' story do with all of his stuff? Does he help other people or use all of his stuff for himself? If you need a hint, look at verses 18-20.

What does God call people who are greedy?

The Treasure:

God gives to us so we can give to others! Money isn't always bad. It's only bad when we want money and stuff more than God! The "rich fool" was given a lot of stuff, but he didn't want to give to others. He was being greedy! Instead of giving to others what he had been given, he built bigger barns for himself.

The Display:

Have you ever given your money or something you had to someone else? How did it make you feel? Has someone ever done that for you? What are ways you can give to others what God has given you?

Lesson 49:
Don't Worry

Key Verses: Luke 12:22-23

And he said to his disciples, "Therefore I tell you, do not be anxious about your life, what you will eat, nor about your body, what you will put on. For life is more than food, and the body more than clothing."

The Map:

When I was going to college in Israel, I had a friend who used to worry about getting sick all the time. The funny thing is that he never did get sick in the four years I knew him! He worried about something that he didn't need to worry about. Sometimes it's easy to get scared about things we really shouldn't be afraid of. In this lesson, Jesus is going to teach us why we don't need to worry.

The Dig: Luke 12:22-34

What does it mean to worry?

What are some things that Jesus says people worry about?

Why does Jesus tell us we shouldn't worry?

What should we be focused on? For a hint, take a look at verse 31.

What does Jesus promise us if we seek to obey Him first?

The Treasure:

Treasure Jesus today and trust Him for tomorrow! God wants us to focus on loving Him each day. When we do this, God promises that He will take care of what we need. There is no need to worry when we are walking with Jesus!

The Display:

How can you focus on treasuring Jesus each day? What can you ask God to help you not worry about?

Lesson 50:
Watch and Work

Key Verses: Luke 12:22-23

And he said to his disciples, "Therefore I tell you, do not be anxious about your life, what you will eat, nor about your body, what you will put on. For life is more than food, and the body more than clothing."

The Map:

Have you ever waited a long time for something? What was it? In the last lesson, we learned that God does not want us to worry. During this lesson, we'll see that Jesus wants us to watch and be ready for His return! He doesn't just want us to watch for Him; He also wants us to work for Him while we are waiting. Let's dig!

The Dig: Luke 12:35-48

How does Jesus want to find us when He returns? Take a look again at verse 37.

Do we know exactly when Jesus will come again? For a hint, look at verse 40.

What does Jesus say some people will do while they are waiting for His return? If you need help, take a look at verse 45.

The Treasure:

Don't just watch, but work for Jesus! Jesus teaches us that when He returns, He will find some people who aren't ready. They will be doing whatever they want to do instead of obeying God. The Bible teaches that Jesus is going to return again someday. He wants us to be ready!

The Display:

How can we be ready for when Jesus returns? Why do you think some people give up watching or waiting for Jesus to return?

Lesson 51:
Divided Over Jesus

Key Verses: Luke 12:22-23

And he said to his disciples, "Therefore I tell you, do not be anxious about your life, what you will eat, nor about your body, what you will put on. For life is more than food, and the body more than clothing."

The Map:

Have you ever had to make a really hard choice? What were you choosing between? In this lesson, we are going to learn how some people will choose to believe in Jesus and some won't. Instead of bringing peace, this will bring division. Let's take a look at what Jesus means in this passage.

The Dig: Luke 12:49-59

What does Jesus say He came to bring?

What example does Jesus use to teach us there will be division?

What does Jesus say they can do? Look again at verses 54-56.

The Treasure:

It is more important to make God happy than it is to make people happy! Jesus knew that living for Him might make other people upset or even mad. As Christians, we know that living for Jesus might cause division. Some people will believe in Him and others won't. It's okay! Live to make God happy.

The Display:

Do you have friends that aren't Christians? Remember that some people aren't Christians because they don't want to be, but others just have never heard about Jesus. Are there friends of yours that you could invite to church or pray for?

The Oasis

Congratulations! You have finished the first volume. I know it was a long journey, but you did it! I hope you have learned a lot about Jesus during this study of Luke. Way to finish strong!

Review Key Verses: Luke 12:22-23

Take a minute and tell your mom or dad the key verses. Remember, you are not allowed to look!

Review Questions:

1. Who does Jesus say we are to pray to?

2. What are some things Jesus mentions we should ask God the Father for?

3. Whose power does Jesus day He was using to defeat evil?

4. What are the Pharisees doing wrong?

5. Why does Jesus tell us not to be afraid of people?

6. What is greed?

7. Why does Jesus tell us not to worry?

The Oasis Activity

FOOD OR CLOTHES?

Put an F next to the items which you think are names of FOOD

Put a C next to the items which you think are names of CLOTHING

LUNGI	CHIMICHANGA	MUESLI
CURRY	ESCARGOT	HANBOK
LEDERHOSEN	KIPPAH	KIMCHI
MUUMUU	DIRNDL	TUNIC
KIPPER	CHEONGSAM	PIEROGI
BERET	BISQUE	TIRAMISU
PASHKA	SAREE	CHAPATI
DASHIKI	CHALUPA	KIMONO

In Closing

Congratulations!

You have finished Luke Volume 1. I hope you continue to enjoy reading and studying the Bible as much as I do. The Bible is not just any normal book. It is God's Word, but it is also God's Story!

The Bible tells us how in the beginning God created the heavens and the earth. Everything and everyone belongs to Him! God created us to live in a loving friendship and relationship with Him. The bad news is that just like Adam and Eve, our sins separate us from God. But the good news is that because God loves us, He sent us a Savior, Jesus, to rescue us from our sins.

John 3:16 says, "For God so loved the world, that he gave his only Son, that whoever believes in him should not perish but have eternal life." The news is that good! When we believe in Jesus, God forgives us of our sins and gives us everlasting life! As Christians, we do not go through life alone. We know that God loves us and is always with us no matter what happens. And best of all, some day we will be together in Heaven with God. Now that is something to look forward to!

I hope you will continue reading and studying God's Word. But most importantly, I pray that as you learn more about God it will help you to love God more. He is truly amazing and worth living for!

There is a lot more to dig for, so be sure to check out Luke Volume 2. It tells the rest of Jesus' amazing story.

Happy Digging,

Doc

Key Terms

Angel: Angels were created by God to be helpers or messengers. They do not have a physical body, but are created spiritual beings.

Chief Priests: These were a group of Jewish leaders who served as priests in the Temple.

Christ (or Messiah): Christ or Messiah means God's anointed or chosen savior. This is Jesus!

Demons: These are bad or evil angels who sinned against God and who now work against God in the world.

Fast (or Fasting): A fast is when someone does not eat and instead focuses on prayer, repentance, and the study of God's Word. Before, and even during the time of Jesus, the Jewish people fasted during the biblical holidays. They would often fast and pray for forgiveness, for God to come and save them, and when they were sad. A fast could last a day, several days, or even several weeks!

Holy Spirit: The Holy Spirit is not just a power or force. He is God, by His power and presence, living in us as Christians. The Bible teaches that God the Father, Jesus, and the Holy Spirit all work together as One.

King Herod: Herod was the King over Judea during the time of Jesus' birth.

Leprosy: Leprosy was a skin disease that caused the Israelites to be unclean according to God's commandments in the Old Testament book of Leviticus. An Israelite with leprosy had to move out of the camp until they were clean.

Pharisees: These people were a group of Jews during Jesus' time who were very concerned with obeying God's commandments. They believed God had given Moses all of these commandments at Mt. Sinai to write for all of the Jewish people to obey. These commandments were called the Written Law and are the first five books of the Old Testament. Not only did they believe God gave Moses these commandments to write down, but they also believed that God spoke other commandments to them that they called the Oral Law. Eventually the Oral Law was written down in a book that is today called the Mishnah.

Repent (or Repentance): Repent means to turn away from sin and turn to God.

Sabbath: Sabbath means "to cease." The Sabbath is a weekly day of rest. It runs from sunset on Friday to sunset on Saturday. It is a special day each week to cease from working and focus on worshipping God.

Sadducees: This was a group of Jewish leaders during the time of Jesus. Most scholars believe they helped to run the Temple in Jerusalem. They had slightly different beliefs than the Pharisees. For example, they only accepted the first five books of the Old Testament, the Written Law, as God's Word. Unlike the Pharisees, they did not believe in the resurrection of the dead, or in angels (Mark 12:18; Acts 23:8).

Satan (or the Devil): Satan, or the Devil, is the leader of all fallen and bad angels.

The Temple: The Temple was a large building, like a church, where the Jewish people worshipped God. It was located in Jerusalem.

About the Author

Patrick Schwenk is a husband, father, and pastor. He is married to Ruth Schwenk, the creator of *The Better Mom* (www.thebettermom.com). They met while attending the Moody Bible Institute in Chicago, Illinois. Pat and his wife have been married for fourteen years and currently have four children ages three to ten.

For additional information on parenting and discipleship resources, visit www.thedigforkids.com and www.thebettermom.com.

Contact Info:

Facebook: www.facebook.com/thedigforkids

Twitter: @patschwenk

The Dig: www.thedigforkids.com

Email: thedigforkids@gmail.com

Design and Artwork:

Cover Design by Design by Insight – www.DesignByInsight.net

Oasis Artwork by Steve Miller - www.torchbearerstudios.com

Edited by Jordy Liz Edits – www.jordylizedits.com

Made in the USA
Lexington, KY
01 March 2017